The Cool of the Day

The Cool of the Day

Poems 1994–2009

by S. C. Fordham

And they heard the sound of the Lord God walking in the garden in the cool of the day, and Adam and his wife hid themselves from the presence of the Lord God among the trees of the garden.

Genesis 3 v. 8

The Cool of the Day this collection 1994–2009 published by S. C. Fordham in 2009
© S. C. Fordham 2009
Preface © Jonathan Fordham 2009

A CIP catalogue record of this book is available in the British library.

ISBN 978-0-9563219-0-9

Designed and produced in the UK by KSD Associates Limited - www.ksdassociates.co.uk

Edited by Jenny Page

Printed in Great Britain by the MPG Books Group, Bodmin and King's Lynn

For information about workshops and poetry readings email Sarah Fordham at
sarah.fordham@btinternet.com

http://blogspot.scfordham.com
www.scfordham.com
www.psalmreadings.com

Regardless of my own beliefs and my own doubts, which are unimportant in this connection, it is my opinion that art lost its basic creative drive the moment it was separated from worship. It severed an umbilical cord and now lives its own sterile life, generating and degenerating itself. In former days the artist remained unknown and his work was to the glory of God. He lived and died without being more than other artisans; 'eternal values', 'immortality' and 'masterpiece' were terms not applicable in his case. In such a world flourished invulnerable assurance and natural humility.

Ingmar Bergman, from his Introduction to
the screenplay of The Seventh Seal

Contents

Preface

As her younger brother, to see the creative output of my talented sister has always given me pleasure and more than a little inspiration. Since Sarah's principal gift, like my own, lies resoundingly in the field of poetry, I must confess this pleasure has at times been mixed with a sense of competition. And in the true manner of sibling rivalry, my 'being proud' at the arrival of Sarah's first book of poetry is swiftly followed by the thought, Darn, you got there first.

Accepting that, the merest glance at the poems collected here reveals a true artist concerned with profound religious and philosophical themes. Sarah consistently presents in her poems a loving God within a Christian framework; for those readers seeking truth in an age obsessed by celebrity, where the media dictates whom we look to for our affirmations, and where the issue of identity is so contested, these poems are valuable currency. The God presented in these poems is neither distant nor an intellectual notion, but emerges from the wellspring of Sarah's heart and experience. He is a God of Truth, Goodness and Beauty. Neither is it a done deal. The struggle towards the light encompasses all the fragility of the human condition. As she says in a poem of the same title: 'I have proclaimed truth's river but have not always been able to swim in it'.

I have also had the privilege of sharing a stage with Sarah as a poet, and to have been in the audience at countless performances, including a notable residency she shared with Sarah de Nordwall at the Poetry Café in the heart of London's Covent Garden. Her ability to turn her hand to set pieces – those contained in this collection are only a suggestion of the depth she has in this area – and to perform poetry set to music and images – reveal another taut string to her bow that might not be obvious from the selection here. Her generosity of spirit, and ability to gather and work graciously with other artists, have been demonstrated over and over in the performance context.

Growing up, I can remember an ancient, battered copy of Tennyson's *Complete Works* being around the house, in which one particular poem, entitled 'Despair', stood out for me and, as she herself has testified, for Sarah too. In fact, she cites this as the poem that got her into all poetry. In that poem the narrator laments being saved from drowning – having made a suicide pact with his wife following the pair's loss of faith. With terrible irony he is saved by the minister of the religious order they had abandoned, to whom the powerful statement is directed: 'But were there a God as you say / His love would have power over Hell till it utterly vanish'd away'. In *The Cool of the Day*, that love has triumphed over adversity through the Cross, so that life becomes a possibility. The poems variously express that fragile but very real hope, enacting the profound truth that 'Beauty / Is asking to be seen / Asking / To be taken inside / And wholly / Loved'. In that act of loving, Hell melts away and the whole world is gained. Sarah's unique voice iterates and reiterates that transaction towards freedom.

Jonathan Fordham, London, July 2009

Introduction

This poetry selection was hard to make. My aim was to choose poems that created a narrative thread weaving through the overarching biblical themes of the Fall, Redemption, Incarnation and Homecoming – both ours and God's – with scenes from my own spiritual journey forming part of the narrative.

Perhaps we can hear God speak to us in 'the cool of the day' through His haunting question to Adam, 'Where are you?', and step out of hiding to face our loving Creator. Guilt, shame, blame, jealousy and murder flowed from that first break in communion and have dogged human existence ever since. It is this pain-filled history, often mirrored in our own lives that Jesus, as the Man of Sorrows, took upon himself as he bore in his own body humanity's curse. The tree Adam stepped out from behind speaks to me of another tree, standing in time and eternity, that shows me the way home.

These poems are some of my moments of reflection on the journey.

Sarah Fordham, London, July 2009

need

we need to come clean
sit out in the autumn rain
let enough water seep through
to float sunken dreams

we need to find the silver thread
weave it through ideals
loop it around as many as possible
make a human wall

we need to dam the tide of hunger
shore up against future's greed
hear hammer blows of tyranny
scales of justice creaking in the breeze

we need our need
we need to see evil's dark heart
and be cut to the bone
we need to come home

July 2007

Speech

Time's cutting edge has carved a deep river
And I, the valley, so remain bowed down
Its flow rushes on through my heart
I dare not look up
Sweeping vanity too much for one body
To carry
Deportment is not dignity
She has gone, blushed red and disappeared
So suddenly

And now the vision tarries
Conspiracy has scaled the walls of man
No one knows, for no one speaks
It comes not from time, wait not in hope
Move against the tide
When the dark sea is reached
You will be gone, turned blue and disappear
So suddenly

I have studied well the temporal line that looks not
At decay nor towards its end
A far horizon, Time the great pretender
Death works, it matters not that you do not look
I look, and tell you what I see
And you smile, turning to ignite the fire of passion
That makes you believe you will not end
Nor have to speak of what you would not see

And here I stay cast down
The rushing river flows as evening comes
It matters not the dimming eyes of youth
Once falling, forever falling into the arms of Time
Is God himself, flesh and bone, bearing every human sin
And emerging from Time's grip
I am made nothing but not wasted
A shattered heart His human hand has gathered in

And I look up
I look up and see the great river streaming like a giant tear
That cuts so deep a path
So deep a truth, it matters not that you will not look
Because whatever course it runs, it runs through you
All of human history is hushed as the river gushes from the side
Of a wound so deep, it becomes a tide of blood
And you are washed, made white, so suddenly

May 2002

Adam and Eve

Where am I in the world?
How did the darkness overtake you and make you something other to
what you were in the beginning?

My source, my bearer, my surround
My strength, my voice, my ground

Your wisdom has gone
And I am separated from my created substance

Reduced to my essential oneness
I have no calling from you

There is no voice to welcome me home
Love is not with you who made me

Even if I could travel back through time
I am for ever shut out

The flaming guardians
The knowledge

The tree from which my mother ate
And my father fled

O
Where am I in the world?

Genesis 3 v. 6

November 2000

Form-ed

From what was I made?
Dark longing of man
Full-orbed hope of woman
Met in yesterday's pool
Where passion rose
And thought descended
Into the deepest depths

From where did I come?
Above, below, within
Womb within a womb
Travelling, entering, confined
Suspended within the walls
Of blind time

What does this mean?
Fallen between
Male and female
Near or thrown far
Distance measuring existence
Beyond maker, creator

Where will I go?
Breath before death
Blame before shame
Brother against brother
A flood, an ark
A flaming sword piercing
Between the light and dark

Genesis 3 v. 24

July 2007

The Cool of the Day

I didn't know where you were
So suddenly departed from your routine
Was it always in your mind
To wander so far from our meeting place?
I didn't know what to do
How long was I to wait?
What was I to think?
I thought our love was real
Strolling through leafy garden glades
Smiling and talking, gazing upon bounty's home

Why did you hide when you heard my footsteps
Approaching among the rustling branches?
The leaves you covered yourself with are withering
My darling, when the sun goes down
You will not be able to find your way home
All this beauty now casts a shadow
I am fading from your memory
And soon you will no longer know who you are
Fading light touches my face tonight
The first of many evenings in, alone

But before you go, take these clothes
Sewn from skins that speak of a sacrifice
Many years from now
A sign, my dearest love
Of how I would allow myself to be hunted down
When you stepped out from behind that tree
I knew I would hang on another
In the cool of a different day
Through the longest of nights
But, right now, I don't want you to be cold

Genesis 3 v. 21

November 2007

6

mourning has broken

the night has broken
morning has arrived
blackbird has spoken
sound of sunlight
praise for war ending
praise for sun rising
praise for life waking
man receives sight

sweet the rain's falling
sunlit my darling
kisses like dewfall
touching my hand
come and remember
our house of sweetness
sprung in completeness
from the first land

mine is the reasoning
mine is the labour
born of the one type
eden expelled
come and forgive us
come and redeem us
need to recover
hand that we held

August 2007

Symbol

I saw a child caught in some branches
And as he struggled to be free
I beheld him for a moment as the face of all children
Now snared in the world
Now fighting to become real
And this child became a living symbol
His hand pushing into the breeze

I saw a woman fall in the street
And as she paused with her head down
I beheld her for a moment as all women
Trying to recover their crown
Trying to establish their dignity
And this woman became a living symbol
Her hand pushing upon the ground

I saw a man waking from a deep sleep
And as he blinked into the day
I beheld him for a moment as the face of all men
Their entry into life
Their speaking the truth
And this man became a living symbol
His hand opened towards the light

1994

He Will Come

The stone gods were immovable to the cries of the woman
Impenetrable to the heart of the man
Indefinable to the movements of the child
With what a reckless imagination have we wrought an image against one
Who calls and seeks in between distance and height, city and ruin,
stillness and war

If love were my master
If beauty my standard
If desolation my pain
If peace were my force
I would look up and see the stars being extinguished one after the other
I would look down and hear the words
'My children, my children, what will become of you
Is there one to come into the powerlessness of this conquered people
and redefine greatness?'

One day the sea will be covered in tiny ships seeking the one destination
Our fathers said it lies beyond the furthest shore
Our mothers said it is closer than these sails flaming in the wind
Our children said, 'No, it is not a place, but a person
Do not seek to the right or to the left
But speak the word, speak the word
And He will come'

Romans 10 v. 8

1995

Some Freedom

My hand reaches up   full of you   In this way the light follows as I tell my
story to those I love   I witness my words running into time and as I draw
breath   I think   it's like releasing birds from a cage   these words of
mine rush up in search of their meanings   It's an undivided quest
and I am powerless to hold captive what longs to be free

There is a great wind gathering   I live for it though I do not feel it now
I lift my hand to catch its first gust   I turn my face to kiss its newness
and I prepare myself to be driven by its force

For how else could I be free?

I go high to look out for some sign   to listen for that sure rumble
travelling in   Though I do not hear it now   I close my eyes in
anticipation   I hold myself in waiting   and I imagine casting myself
upon its strong wings

For how else could I be free?

I watch the sun disappear again   and as the night deepens I stand even
stiller   I strain for that great movement   the tremendous sound
I say over and over   I am here   knowing no other way to be found

For how else could I be free?

1996

Calm Surface

Where am I in the world?
How can I find home?
Is it a house by the sea?
Above in the clouded sky?
To the foothills?
Beyond the plains?
The peaceful field?
The mountain range?
In the deep heart of a cave I will be waiting to be given as a promise
To hold in my arms the wind and the rain
All of nature waiting with me
There is something to be revealed
What is it?
Can I reach through the brightness of the sun to exist in the light?
Can I plant myself like a tree in water and live on the earth changing through
the seasons?
Why does it not come?
Where is the good soil?
How is it the darkness advances and wars still rage?
The world a calm surface before the storm
I witness the sea beating the rocks and the withering of time in a hundred faces
My brother, my mother, my sister, my father, my friend, where is my country?
Why does love not die?
Is it not blown away like the falling leaves of autumn?
Who strengthens me?
Who comforts me when I am alone?
Who could break through the calm of this surface to bear the storm?
Will the world die as slowly as a tree when all the water has gone?
A great winter comes
Who will lead me through the mountains and the snow?
Who will build me a house, a place to rest, give me peace as a river?
Who tells me not to fear?
Who gives me strength?
Who comforts me when I am alone?
Where is my home?
The leaves have fallen
Why does love not die?

In the withering of time a hundred faces, a hundred strangers
What is my number?
Who will call my name?
How will it endure, my name and the hundred others?
Winter will come again
One hundred other mornings to break the calm surface of night
Who will bear the storm?
How can I pierce the brightness to live in warmth and light?

Who is my brother?
Who is my mother?
Who is my sister?
Who is my father?
Who is my friend?
Where is my country?
Where is my home?
He who made the earth
When will it become His own?

1998

Who? Where? When? Why? What?

The Singer's song untaught
unuttered, unknown
by so many
yet deeply understood
by naked humankind
is the mystery of the Word
laid bare . . .

Shame-filled fingers tremble
Lips move
The beginning of prayer
is mourning over
uttered sin

Stricken nights fall from me
and dew-filled mornings sweep away
dawn's doubts

Who calls?
Where is the hand to hold me?
When will the students of destruction
be stopped?
Why can't I find him whom my soul loves?

What covers me?
Hiding the gift from the giver
Giving the gift like it's mine
What folly

Who is rising?
Where have I fallen?
When do I arrive?
Why have you gone?
What comes?

Can I hold your gaze for a lifetime?
Face to face
In shallow waters and in the depths
In nothing and in everything
In vulnerability and in strength

What is it I want?
What is my choice?

My will is a knife to pierce
the membrane of fate
and turn the world on its edge

And turn me to face the Beloved
and not look down; not ever
To grasp the hand of
faith and hope

and live

Song of Solomon 3 v. 1

April 2009

One Morning

One morning I rose early enough to speak with the World. She said to me, 'The turning of my body moves you on and on you go. I cannot help except give you Time . . .'

Time came to my door one night and gave me his coat to wear. 'The more you wear it, the closer it will fit, and when it is worn through, one day, I will return to claim it back. I cannot help you except introduce you to Destiny . . .'

Destiny used to sit under my window and laugh. 'You think I'm real, you think I make you, but really you make me, you make me. I cannot help you except show you Reason . . .'

Reason took me by the hand one night as a storm raged outside and said, 'I can calm you, but do not build on me. My sister is called Tragedy, build on her . . .'

Oh, she would often come and sit and talk with me. 'I visit many,' she said, 'but am never welcome, so I move on. I cannot help you except give you Strength. But I have heard of another, one who, some say, gathers in the lost and shows them the most beautiful of people. They say she is called Forgiveness . . .'

I went with Strength through many cities, asking if anyone could tell me where she lived, but after many days, Strength left me . . .

It was then three persons approached holding up their hands as if in triumph. 'We are Truth,' they said. 'Come with us; we have much to show you, but first let us introduce you to our dear friend. He is called Redemption . . .

They let go of the middle one's hand and he came towards me. 'Here', he said, 'is Forgiveness . . .'

Her fragile beauty was haunting as she smiled down upon my years of searching. It was as as if through her gaze she was making them her very own. I will not forget her words . . .

'Here are the ones I love the most. No matter what happens to you, they will never leave you.' She raised her one hand. 'This one is Joy.' And then the other, 'and this one, Peace.'

1996

'But above all things truth beareth away the victory' *Plato*

Speak through the heat, haze and hubris
Sound just one word
Food for a wayward journeyer
Caught
Upon foreign planes
Within distant memories

I couldn't tell you why I went outwardly so far
When inwardly there was only one spot to stand upon
And weep
To remain so still within yet be moving and moving
Across fields and cities, in sunshine, snow and rain
Tell me, why did I not wait for the early morning dew?

Moments came and went
Fleeting little things so briefly alighting
I couldn't ever catch one
Not even once
But how, how could it be
With my candle and my cross and a bleeding heart
I could ever be imprinted with evening song?

Definition enough, enough now
For a moment falls from the sky
Like a falling star
Full of death, full of belonging, full of fire
Tell me, how could it be that I should make
Such a trilogy part of me?

Lightwards was not only above
But emanating from a pierced heart
And a translucent side
Rough wood catches me most nights
Between majesty and awakening
Beholding and flowering ...

And Beauty
Is asking to be seen
Asking
To be taken inside
And wholly
Loved

Genesis 27 v. 28

April 2009

Godhead

1

Great Word please – sound in me now
If there is a word then there must be a voice
And if there is a voice then there must be a thought
And a thought must have the womb of a mind to protect and conceive
Great Word please – I am dying for sense

2

It was a gift. My heart was full not of my own thoughts but of one
thought only; and this was God's. One day He spoke this thought and it
became a Word. I have spoken many words and they are like offspring –
sons of my many thoughts. God spoke just once and His Word was truly
His offspring, His only Son. As you look up through my words to
understand me, look up through God's Word to understand Him. By the
speech of eternity being translated into the language of time, my language
of time becomes eternal speaking.

3

Gone is the great distance
In which death's hand was held before me like a mirror
And desolation had a shape that was mine
I looked for truth but found none
I listened for some fellowship and heard only one voice that did not echo
I thought, I am a message not to be taken
I stand on this great plain with no guide

Gone is the great distance in which I saw only myself
Because into the line of time God became man
He took the hand of death and as he stood before me

Desolation became his shape
I saw his truth
I heard his voice and it carried such a distance, it's being carried still
I received his message and it became me

The great plain entered me
And as it became eternity
He became my guide

And now gone is the great distance

John 1 v. 18

February 2002

I Call to Thee

I call to Thee
I hasten the time when you will speak
And all my emptiness will be filled
The tide of my advancing years will retreat
And at last I will behold the face
The one I love
The one for whom I count all things as loss

All things as nothing to compare with thee
When all your riches you let go to clasp such a hand as mine
And this fallen world to hold you were so sent
To stand in my place and take nothing you deserved
A poor man's punishment

For by what were the nails that pierced your hands so driven?
By hate? By fear? One bitter word?
For what act of love were your feet fixed so as not to move?
O, I call to thee
I call

But no, defeated not, but I
Defeated yet still living
And you the one who died
Death held not
But given up to live a second time
And so for ever

I call to thee
I hasten the time when you will speak
And all emptiness will be filled
The tide of the advancing years will retreat
And at last all will behold the face
The face of love
The one who for us counted all things as loss

All things as nothing to compare
To clasp such a hand as this
Hold a world so fallen
Nothing you deserved
Such a punishment
The bitter words
The act of love
The fixing of the feet
Defeated
Dying
Dead
But rising
Given up
Not you but I
Alive for ever more
I call to thee
O it is to thee I call

Philippians 3 v. 7

2000

Entrance: The Light

When the Light came into the world things were never to be the same again. This Light took a body just like us and said, *I have seen all people in all times and now I am near.* This was a light unlike any other. A candle shines for a while then completely disappears. A lamp burns brightly and then runs dry. The sun goes down every day and sometimes the moon does not even appear. A match illuminates for only a few short seconds. Many have asked throughout the centuries, where is the Eternal Flame? There is one by your side this very minute saying, *I am the Light that gives light to you. I am love made alive. I am the toiler, the builder of your dreams . . .*

I Timothy 6 v. 16
John I vs 4–5

1999

No Room

House full
Door shut
Lock and key
To keep in the old
Exclude the new

Ban possibility

Pale light smoulders
Shadows lengthen
No invite
But a star is high
A way unfolds

Drive on dark night

No room
No welcome
Such a long ride
Baby born
This cold eve

Outside

Luke 2 v. 7

November 2008

Winterval

It's so cold here in Winterval
Shop lights glow revealing treasures within
Calling across empty hearts where sorrow hides
'There's more, always more
Come inside'

It's so silent here in Winterval
Like the little match girl freezing in the last flicker of dawn
We wait to be found
No star in the night, no chorus of angels
No word spoken, no: not a sound

It's so dark here in Winterval
They took down every sign
No welcoming inn to rest a while, no sweet wine to savour
Made like barren women, never to give birth, always to strive
Like men, for ever to journey, but never to arrive

It's so sad here in Winterval
With no reason to give gifts
We lie wrapped in a joyless world, so meek, so mild
Nothing to remember, no story to tell
No Christ to worship and adore, just an inner child

*The name Winterval was the result of an attempt by a UK city council
to rename Christmas*

Matthew 2 v. 11

November 2007

Son

Such an irregular descent, who can know?
Godhead reduced to a seed
Planted in virgin territory, to grow
And emerge gasping for air
Such a tiny hand clasping a finger
And she, looking down amazed, whispering
'My Son, from where did you come?'

Such an adoption, who can imagine?
Betrothed, loving, desiring to cover all shame
Flames of fire in the night camping around evil's lure
Entrusted to protect the world's saviour
When you watched him working with wood
Did your eyes fill with wonder as you whispered
'My Son, from where did you come?'

Such a journey, who would undertake?
To follow a star, to be led to a child, to worship the king
Then to find a different way home
Fine-robed, under a clear night's sky
Three men alone with their thoughts, staring ahead
A whisper carrying on the wind
'Son of God, from where did you come?'

And as I ask, the question hangs in the air before taking off
I must follow and gain wings to keep up
The flight of faith – to dwell within a childlike trust
A humble obedience, and the journey
Who knows where I'll go?
Son of Man, you made this your home
Filled up for my lack, and took a different way back

Matthew 2 v. 12

August 2005

26

The Great Awakening

Half the earth starving lit in neon
A peace to keep in this turning world
One man's dream – storm or sun
Changed in sleep

Changed – the rugged distance – the snow-capped mountains
The lonely haunts of wild beasts – the empty table – the grieving mother
The child who only looks and does not speak

The peace of one man's dream
No storm to move – no sun to wither it away
In waking it remained and he was washed in the sea every night
Until he was crucified closed his eyes and died

Through the blue sky the raw heat of the sun
The frozen waste of its absence
Universal solemnity – universal eternity
Planets spinning – the distress of rocks hurtling through space

And then it comes – the great cornerstone
Adding flesh – sinew – bone
To make a footprint in the desert sand
And then to walk into town like that – a man

Sick men rise – no more the cover of night to hide
Everything changed – the first last – the weak strong
The greatest has become the servant of all

And then we learned the things we held as most important were really
of no account at all
As the widow showed as the coin dropped from her hand – and Judas
turned and went into the night
Silver in his fist – the Field of Blood spread out – in the end the Lord of all
Betrayed not for money but by a kiss

And humanity hurls on its way
The heap of war – blood draining from lips
That kiss – a promise that never held
Flesh felled in the field where Judas hangs as a pendulum swinging in time

The spit on the cheek
The truth I didn't speak
The widow and Judas
Her empty hand – his body marking time

Lips that begin to move in prayer
Changed in sleep
Jesus Christ – Son of God – our Saviour
Are there only the tombs of men in which to rest?

Has only the tomb of God been emptied?
The rolled stone marking death's last stop
Changed in sleep
Jesus Christ – Son of God – our Saviour

The Great Awakening comes

And changed – the rugged distance – the snow-capped mountains
The lonely haunts of wild beasts – the empty table – the grieving mother
The child who only looks and does not speak

Sick men rise – no more the cover of night to hide
Everything changed – the first last – the weak strong
The greatest has become the servant of all

Mark 12 vs 41–44
Matthew 27 vs 1–8

2000

Out of the Mist

I held within the Saviour of the world
And walked, step by step, into the unknown
Blood and cries gave birth to Him
And as I saw myself in those dear eyes
I knew now there were different stars to behold
Other treasures to find . . .

As He grew, a tree sometimes cast a shadow across my path
Memories would return: His tiny hand clasping my finger
Him labouring in the workshop
Handling wood, pausing to talk to me
Such skilled hands that were to reach out
To those no one would touch . . .

My boy
I could not protect Him from those hate-filled looks
Murderous whispers and a jeering crowd
I could not take Him back inside
Overshadowed by rough wood
This time the blood and cries were His . . .

And as darkness fell
He spoke from out of the mist
I could barely understand it then
Giving me another family
John's strong arm supporting me
As I stumbled and wept
Remembering the words I spoke at the beginning of it all . . .

My soul does magnify the Lord and my spirit does rejoice in God my Saviour . . .

Luke I vs 46–55

December 2004

Man of Sorrows

My hand trembles for You in a world that has covered its shame.

The night wind moves the trees and I am no longer my own.

I do not know where I am going, so I'll go as the wind blows.

North, south, east, west, You are my compass, my circumference,
my bright morning star.

Your words are like brave soldiers standing on the battlefield ready
to die to save me.

The darkness comes, and it is enough to cover myself with Your flesh
and blood.

Remembering You in this mist, my cup is overflowing.

Your body hanging in time, a vertical sacrifice, I lift my face to You.

My eyes search Your wounds for a place to hide, to rest.

Your hands, Your feet, Your head, I stop at Your broken heart, and let the
water flowing from Your side wash me.

My iniquity is revealed, Your thorny crown becomes my funeral wreath.

I am as ashes dispersing in the wind and I am gone, never to return, until I
rise with you.

Together we walk the ruins, kick up the dirt until we strike the foundation.

Your pierced hand my glove, I cannot measure myself against You.

I have become limitless in Your sorrow.

Isaiah 53 v. 3
Psalm 103 v. 14

2000

30

Entire

It was complete what you did
When you hung your head and there was no more thought
I was left with only trust, like a knife, to empty my heart's excess
And make it hollow –
Entire without its lonely centre, without what had been done to me
Without what I had performed –
Head lowered, eyes shut

It was enough to feel your shame
Naked indulgence streaking across your skin
And when they cut you, your torn flesh could now fill my dark space within
And you grew inside me like you did inside your mother's womb –
The birth was completed
Blood and sweat marking out my place –
In straw, with strangers, with you

The star was not the star of fortune
Prominence has sunk unto some riverbed
I have no face to present myself secure
Sparrows, lilies in the field, wisdom like Solomon's –
Forces me out
Entire without my past, a stream my path –
Drawing water up through my feet

To water what has been left to rot and waste
It could never be enough
Human existence falling through the years to meet me
Unprepared and incomplete –
Until I met your broken form, merging God with the very structure
Of sin that engineered me, made me this –
And gripped the world in war, in want

The massacre of the innocents just goes on
World rulers with Herod's eyes look upon the young and see themselves
Guilty and not bearing it, a knife betrays the heart's excess
I watch, I speak, I turn upon my dreams –
To find the way that would lead to peace
A Prince? What coronation was foretold in that stable –
Did the thorns in the eyes of your Father, as he watched the scene, make
Him weep?

To become one with the world's suffering, with me
A strange destiny stirring within a baby's tiny form
A child throughout my childhood years, a boy dancing in the street
Learning in the temple, leaning on your mother's breast, your father's arm –
The time gathering pace towards the final sacrifice
To bear in your body now full grown, the ultimate desecration –
Evil's genius and God's master plan

What does this mean as the planet spins, suspended in my eyes?
The earth you walked, I walk, I try to follow your footprints in the desert
In the sands of my misfortune
Your heart pulses on –
Through the heights, the depths, and between my soul and the world's
outer edge –
There you are

Matthew 2 v. 16

2003

the centre of sorrow

ripples on a surface expanding
the edge not seen
a stone dropped from a great height
the depth not fathomed

plummeting pebble of yesterday
sinking still
seeking the centre of sorrow
falling, falling

through all those soundless places
o if i could see
if i could know
if i could grasp

the pierced hand
delving to catch
this weighted
pain-filled thing

and swallow it down
drowning the swathes
of darkness
that fostered such a child

and there it is
transfigured and blessed body
containing sorrow's centre
how could you ingest this most bitter pill

and not die again?
once and for all
a heartbeat ceased
blood and water flowed

forgive me
if i cannot stand
on the banks
of fathomless love

where there's no edge
no bottom
no end
to be swept where by the tide?

Encompassed
But truly
For ever
Yours x

Romans 6 vs 9–11

August 2008

The Fourth Watch of Night

I will not forget taking John's body past the temple guards
His head having been served on a silver platter
To satisfy an appetite beyond my imagination
We buried him in silence and then returned to tell our master

I will not forget the look of grief that swept over him
He seemed diminished in stature as he turned away
I watched his figure get smaller as he rowed his boat to a solitary place
But before long so many people left what they were doing –

Walked right on out from the cities to be where he was, and we followed
And I watched as the grief of my master changed into compassion
As he lifted up his eyes to see the crowd that had gathered
I will not forget how he seemed to grow so tall as he rose to heal the sick

His eyes shining a love beyond my imagination
When evening came we were all so tired and wanting to send each back
to their home
But he said no, they do not need to go, you give them something to eat
Perhaps he was remembering John's head on that silver platter –

Five loaves and two fishes to satisfy the appetite of 5,000 men
And when he blessed the food he did not look down and close his eyes
as other men
But lifted his whole countenance to the sky
I will not forget how he broke the loaves –

A far cry from our Last Supper
How could we then have known what was to come
The giving of his body so all men could eat
And never be hungry again

But in this amazing scene we picked up twelve full baskets left over
When he told us to go on before him
So he could at last be alone to talk to his Father
I watched him disappear into the hills, and there he stayed under the
cover of night

Many miles from the land the wind turned against us
I felt such fear as we were beaten and tossed by the waves
I thought of my master so calm and strong
And it was in the fourth watch of night that he came to us

Walking on the water
Our screams carried on the wind
But louder returned the words
Take courage, it is I, do not be afraid

I asked him to call for me
And so it was that I stepped out of the boat
To walk as he walked
Stepping over the waves

I would have done anything to reach him in that moment
But when the wind blew again I felt such fear
And cried out for him to save me
I was sure I was going to drown

But even as I uttered the words he caught me and asked me
why I doubted
I knew as never before this was God's true Son
I did not forget this even as I heard the crowing of the cock
But still I think of how it must have been for him

His dear cousin John
The crowds that always thronged about him
The times alone he prayed under a clear night's sky
The sick he healed

The hungry he fed
And when he died
I will never forget that I had denied him
And how he always knew what I was made of

As the wind blows upon the waters of this world
I strain to hear his words again, Take courage, it is I . . .
His hand holding me in the dark
The depths below me

And I think again how it was for him
Who was there in his fourth watch when he cried
My God, my God why . . .?
And then when my master died

I could not reach him
Nor be to him as he was to me
I still feel the grip of his hand in the hour of my greatest need
And I weep, thinking of our little boat driven and tossed by the wind

Mark 6 vs 14–55

2003

Poppy

Grown in such inhospitable ground
Petals of pity trembling in battle's breeze
Pity for all that's lost, for all in the grip of blind force
Pity for every soul torn, for the weight of unrelenting remorse
Distressed soil of forgotten fields your home

The earth weeping the blood in which your seed is sown
Pick the poppy, make its death your own
Wear it close to your heart, walk on
But do not look for peace
It is the shoes on your feet

Ephesians 6 v. 15

July 2007

A fisherman, when he casts his angle into the river, doth not throw the hook in bare, naked and uncovered, for then he knows the fish will never bite, and therefore he hides the hook within a worm, or some other bait, and so, the fish, biting at the worm, is catched by the hook. Thus Christ, speaking of himself, saith, I am a worm and no man. He, coming to perform the great work of our redemption, did cover and hide his Godhead within the worm of his human nature. The grand water serpent, Leviathan, the devil, thinking to swallow the worm of his humanity, was caught upon the hook of his divinity. This hook stuck in his jaws, and tore him very sore. By thinking to destroy Christ, he destroyed his own kingdom, and lost his own power for ever.

Lancelot Andrews writing about Psalm 22 v. 6, quoted from p. 339, *The Treasury of David* by Charles Spurgeon

The Way

The night has come
But it is nothing to the darkness in my heart

Like wax, it is as if melted within me

I walked dusty streets and shared the burdens of men
And now my feet will not move

My bones, as if all out of joint

Who will take me home ...
And as my hands are stretched about me
Who will lead me on ...

Poured out, as if like water

I descend

Not as a man, as if a worm

And now as my Father turns

I am torn

Psalm 22

2004

Psalm 23 Trilogy

I

The Lord is my Big Brother
I am never alone
His eye is on me round the clock
He speaks to me
Sits me down in a dead comfy chair
And asks me about my day
Takes a real interest
And leads me to places I never thought I'd go
Now I'm in His house –
It's rent-free and he'll never evict me . . .
It's well secure here
He's built a wall to keep the enemy out
The door's locked
And he's given me the key!
I can come and go as I please
And he's right there –
Shoulder to shoulder
Step by step
Eyeball to eyeball
On the level
With me

2

The Lord is my shepherd
I shall not want, want, want
To be outside of your pasture
A wandering beast alone
Looking for water
Soul torn

The Lord is my shepherd
I shall not want, want, want
To stumble on a rocky path
Upholding my name
Only my shadow cast
Unaware I'm headed for the valley
Of no way through and of no return

The Lord is my shepherd
I shall not want, want, want
To cower under cover of darkness
Comfortless, boundaryless
The enemy having feasted in my home
The doors left swinging on their hinges
The table strewn with empty plates
And glasses all turned upside down

The Lord is my shepherd
I shall not want, want, want
Joylessness and an empty cup
Followed by the ghosts of the past
The withered grass of the field woven through
All the days of my life
All my nights
Through all my longing for quiet and desire
In rain, storm, flood or fire

All the days of my life
To dwell only in the circle of my eyes
And after I'm gone
My house left to rack and ruin
The Lord is my shepherd
I shall not want, want, want

3

The Lord is my shepherd
I hear your voice, you make my path safe to tread upon

I shall not want
You care is perfect, knowing what I need even before I ask

He makes me to lie down in green pastures
As I rest in your word, you make me like a strong tree

He leads me beside the still waters
You pour out your Spirit, watering my roots

He restores my soul
As you cover me with your wings, you heal me

He leads me in the paths of righteousness
You lead me forth

For His name's sake
Not me now Lord, but you

*Yea, though I walk through the valley of the shadow of death, I will fear
no evil, for You are with me*
When the darkness overtakes me and death stalks close, shoulder to
shoulder you walk with me, so I am not afraid . . .

Your rod and Your staff, they comfort me
Rule my life, Lord, give me counsel, so that I would be strengthened

You prepare a table before me in the presence of my enemies
Thank you for your provision! I have peace in your constant victory

You anoint my head with oil
My great high priest

My cup runs over
There is nothing more I need now, save you

Surely goodness and mercy shall follow me all the days of my life
To the one who supplies my need and covers my sin, I give you thanks ...
Only your blessing, behind me, overtaking me ... O Lord ...

And I will dwell in the house of the Lord for ever
In life and in death, I am yours

June 2007

I have proclaimed truth's river but have not always been able to swim in it

I tried to hear the voice of love in the midst of the world's empty spinning.

I tried to listen to the only one who can save – the only one mighty enough to deliver from deep darkness.

God of heaven came down and walked through the haze of sinfulness, The cloud of sorrowfulness, upon the shards of forgetfulness, and reached the edges of me.

Some will call, open-handed, shame-faced, contrite, while others will remain tight shut.

Those who do not open their eyes unto vain shallow tidings and cover themselves with truthful writings – they are the ones who will be blessed!

The Lord has taken the beating, the whipping, the driving pain of nails through flesh and bone.

He does not need silence, empty chatter or pretence.

He does not need the deep shaft of injustice reaching down into his earth.

I say, 'When will the dark corners be exposed by the ruthless searchlight from on high?

So many cowering figures to unfold, and my heart's story yet to be told.'

I have proclaimed truth's river but have not always been able to swim in it.

Lord, will you not destroy the giants of corruption tramping through the mazes of indifference?

Concrete and steel columns that seem immovable will crack from within and crumble upon the heads of the poor.

Swirling patches of darkness like typhoons will rush down and catch men up, along with the things that they have made.

And I remain fixed in a closed space surveying my hands and the landscape for new signs of life.

Lord, there is the enemy who comes only to rob, kill and destroy.

Broken vessels are strewn upon the earth.

Lord, when will you lead the heavenly host out?

When will the gate swing wide and prosperity shout?

Lord, you stand on the edge of victory's dawn, as so many hearts are failing.

My eyes are dimming.

The ravages of sin have made so much of the earth uninhabitable.

Yet it is still lived in.

Lord of hosts, this is your home.

Psalm 40

December 2007

He Did Not Grasp

He did not hold on . . .
His hands freed
To be nailed
To the rough wood
Of man's own power . . .
A stake in the ground

He did not regard . . .
His reputation ripped from Him
Like the skin from His back
Tied to the post
Of man's own will . . .
A stake in the ground

He did not grasp . . .
But let go to walk as a man
His feet freed to bleed
On the cross
Of man's own thought about himself . . .
A stake in the ground

Philippians 2 v. 6

2003

The Snowdrop

A tear before falling
Held in fragility
Overcoming the winter
The flower to spring forth first
From the darkness of the earth

A pure promise of spring
Clothed in simplicity
Shivering in the wind
An eldest child longing for many brothers –
For a sudden appearing, a carpet of beauty

From highest heaven He came
Feet planted on rough wood
He died in the deepest of winters
The firstborn of many brethren
The third day to spring forth

What does this mean?
Praying and pleading
Fallen man upon a frozen earth
So many not seeing the white bud pushing up
Breaking winter's curse

The firstfruits of creation
Asking for others to come and to cover
The earth in beauty beyond all despair
Many brethren, many brethren suddenly appearing
Creation is singing, the melting, the melting's begun

Romans 8 v. 29

February 2006

The Blossom is Falling from the Trees

The blossom is falling from the trees
      Sailing down on high winds to a low tide
How love ebbs and flows, bringing back
Voices, mixed tones and human silence
      The birds chirp and call and cover each other in spring
The brush of their wings wiping memories from me –

The blossom is falling from the trees
      Strange spring snow floating, falling, with me feeling
Shifting earth within heart and under heel
Wrapped in winter's cloak so late
      Too late to remember what there is to forget
Now that only dreaming sees

The blossom is falling from the trees
      A season's full circle hems me round
Enough now! The thread is tight
Memories, taut, spring back and hide for ever in deep soil
      The West Country – all my earth, all my birdsong
As mixed tones are now silenced and white-shaded –

As the blossom, faded from my vision dresses me entirely
      Closed eyes, I hear another voice and am awakened
He's come! The Bridegroom riding high, bending low
To dust the blossom from my brow
      He clasps my hand, and whispers
'Rise my love, my fair one, come away with me' –

The blossom has fallen from the trees
　　　Cherries come through wood and bark
A gentle breeze, high tide
At last! Fruit to bend the bough
　　　Sprung forwards, a vision of tomorrow's song
And the blossom, the blossom is all gone –

Song of Solomon 2 v. 10

2005

Why do you look for the living among the dead?

The question hangs in the air before touching me
In the depths of my soul
Why have I been perplexed when peace stands so near?
Why have I not been dazzled daily by the light of the world?
Why have I been still afraid when you say there is nothing to fear?

'Remember,' whispers a voice
'How he spoke to you,
Return from the tomb!
He is not there! Nor ever shall be!'

Out of the many words that I speak
In prayer may some rise to the heavens . . .
In faith may others believe what I say, run to that tomb
And see for themselves linen wrappings fallen to the ground
And marvel as they journey towards home

Luke 24

March 2009

ELEMENTAL

EARTH	In the soil I cover myself
FIRE	Rubbing sticks to make a spark
WATER	And later in the warmth of the water
AIR	I breathe deeply
LIFE	Rivers springing eternal from within this earthen
	vase

John 7 v. 38

August 2001

Moment

1
In the fullness of time it came
Like a butterfly pausing a moment on my hand
Only a resting-place
I breathe in and then out
And then it is gone
Beauty and fragility and fullness

2
Beautiful and fragile
Not knowing a fellow creature
Wings like paper
To live, to pause, to rest, to utter softly
A moment given
A fellow creature, a resting-place

3
In the fullness of time it came
Beautiful and fragile

Like a butterfly pausing a moment on my hand
Not knowing a fellow creature

Only a resting-place
Wings like paper

I breathe in and then out
To live, to pause, to rest, to utter softly

And then it is gone
A moment given

Beauty and fragility and fullness
A fellow creature, a resting-place

2002

everything depends upon the rain

everything depends upon the rain
rushing, pouring, trickling, spitting
down, down
everything depends upon the soft drops
penetrating hard earth
finding the roots

everything depends upon standing outside
in the downpour
being soaked to the skin
and within
a deep well bubbles up
and laughs

everything scorched
everything bitten by dust
everything withered
and dried up
soaked, soaked

everything depends upon the rain
the rain, rain
falling down, falling fast
falling between us
and within our hearts

Deuteronomy 32 vs 1–3

April 2009

Homecoming

The earth will give birth to her dead and disclose the blood shed upon her
She will conceal the slain no longer
In that day a great trumpet will sound
And those perishing, those in exile, will come, will come and worship

The day when God comes –

Hail will sweep away lies
Water will overflow every hiding place
Agreement with the grave will no longer stand
And I will weep no more

Wherever I turn I will hear a voice telling me which way to walk
There will be rain for the seed I sow
And streams of water will flow on every high mountain and hill
The moon will shine like the sun
And the light will be seven times brighter like the light of seven full days

When God comes –

Every stammering tongue will be fluent when the desert becomes
a fertile field
And every fertile field will be seen like a forest
And at last I will live in quietness and confidence
My fearful heart is spoken to: 'Be strong, do not fear'

God comes –

And the blind see
The deaf hear
The lame leap like deer
The mute shout
As water flows

As God comes –

And instead of burning sand, a pool
In the haunts where the jackal once lay, grass and reeds will grow
A highway will be there
The way of holiness where the redeemed will walk
Where the ransomed will return

Every valley raised
Every mountain made low
Rough ground levelled
Rugged places plain

When God comes –

Strength to the weary
The power of the weak increased

To soar on wings like eagles
To run and not grow weary
To walk and not faint

When God comes –

Rivers to overflow on barren heights
Parched ground into springs
Trees in the desert
Pines in the wasteland
And I, a bruised reed
I, a smouldering wick
Never to be broken, snuffed out

My darkness turns into light
And in my blindness I am led
Guided along unfamiliar paths
Where the waters will not sweep over me
The fire will not burn me

My family scattered in the earth gathered
Brought from afar
Delivered from the ends of the earth
When God comes –

The treasures of darkness will be given to me
Riches stored in secret places
I will be strengthened from the sun's rising to the place of its setting
And I will know there is no other God like the God who does not speak
in secret
Who makes my sun never to set
My moon to wane no more
And my days of sorrow to end

And at last beauty, not ashes
Gladness, not mourning
Praises, not despair

When God comes –

Never again will there be an infant who lives only a day
Or a man who does not live out his years
Never again will I build a house for others to live in
Or grow food for others to eat

When God comes –

As the days of a tree
So will my days be

When God comes –

Home

Isaiah 26 v. 9

1998

Pure Steel

The flashing blade
Will blind the enemy's eye
For a moment in time

The advantage gained
Sure-footed on the Rock
With a firm grip

Thrust forward the Spirit's sword
The pure steel will not fail
Jesus is Lord

Hebrews 4 v. 12

2007

Stay

Why do you leave, my love?
Where do you go?
It's cold outside
And soon there'll be snow . . .

Stay here with me, my love
I have all you need
The warmth of my gaze will heal you
My precious bruised reed . . .

I've counted your sorrows
I've watched from afar
So now that you're here
Let me be your bright morning star . . .

There's no welcome out there
There's nothing to say
Except stay here with me, my love
Please, don't go away . . .

A lover's heart broken
Tears in the night
Not knowing where you'll lay your head
Only the horizon in sight . . .

So stay here with me, my love
Without fruit, what is the vine?
There's so much before us
Please say you'll be mine . . .

John 15 v. 4

July 2005

Dust and Ashes

I have the right not to touch
Not to go forward
To pull the past like a blanket over me
And to stay here like water in a glass

I have the choice to touch
To go forward
To cast off the past and arise
And to run, run like the wind

I have the right to remember
To hold memory like a sword to slay the future
To strike at the heart of possibility
And to stay here disappearing, like water poured out on the ground

I have the choice to forget
To wield memory like a sword to slay the past
To strike at the heart of repetition
And to become visible in the early morning light

I have the right not to become anything
To remain shrouded in Time's cloak, trying to make it stop

I have the choice to become something
To wear Time's cloak, crafting something in the hours given to me

I have the right to turn from my brother
Kill my lover with silence
Ignore my mother
And echo my father's fear

I have the choice to turn towards my brother
Speak to my lover
Embrace my mother
And silence my father's fear

I have the right not to be free
To be suspended in amniotic fluid
An embryo never to pierce the world with a cry

I have the choice to become free
To be born again
Pierce the world with a cry of greeting

I have the right to be numb
And to stay here
Like water absorbed into the earth

I have the choice to feel
To follow the wind that blows
To be made manifest

I have the choice to live for ever

I have the right to rest in peace

Genesis 18 v. 27

April 2002

Sequence

the darkened edges
bruised reeds, a smouldering wick
hope springs eternal

hope springs eternal
bruised reeds, a smouldering wick
the darkened edges

underworld return
turning the shadows of night
to glorious light

Isaiah 42 v. 3

July 2007

Love is . . .

love is quiet
riding the stillness
seeking rest
finding its voice
but to listen
to hear
bow down
bow down now
and blow the dust away
from those travelling shoes

I John 4 v. 8

2000

The Path of Meaning

These were dangerous times, especially for the servants of the Word. They were looked down upon, despised, persecuted by others and killed by some. And all for correct pronunciation.

Word had lived upon the middle of the earth once, and when He spoke, people would block their ears and shout. Correct pronunciation hadn't been heard for such a long time, He was hated for it and eventually they killed Him. There were some, though, who listened in wonder at His speech as if it were music. They were so sad to see Him die such a terrible, undeserving death.

However, death wasn't the end for Word because, as with all words, there is a preceding thought, and all thought and language contains within it the power of creative action. It was because of the greatest idea ever thought that Word came back to life, just for a short time, before disappearing from amid a puzzled crowd of onlookers and loved ones.

In the times that followed it was only those who longed for words to be pronounced correctly who discovered this Union of Thought, Word and Power. As a sign of Union's pleasure at being able to share Himself, He gave Power as a special gift to the Meaning Speakers. This gave them the ability to speak in other languages not understood with their minds. When going through hard times, and it was difficult to think, this ability renewed their strength. But the most wonderful thing of all about Union's special gift of Power was that it meant the Meaning Speakers always knew the conversation happening in the heart of Union. And how they loved to talk! This made everything worthwhile.

You see, it wasn't all good news. There was a grand enemy, known in the popular imagination as Media King. It was only the Meaning Speakers who knew his real name – the Prince of the Power of the Air, Father of Lies. People looked to Him to give them Meaning. His message was simple: 'Let Meaning be whatever you want it to be. You decide!' The most popular name for his kingdom was The Place of Mirrors because day and night there was great rejoicing in reflection and projection. Only the Meaning Speakers knew its real name – the Branded Kingdom, for all living in it were marked.

The Meaning Speakers had a real fight on to come out of the Branded Kingdom because all were born into it and, during the time of the Earth Age, had to live within its walls. Now, there were certain times when Meaning was revealed, and these were known as Moments of Clarification to some, and the Greater Delusion to others, depending on the heart's orientation towards or away from Meaning. Soon after these times a special ceremony would be held called Upholding. In some areas within the Branded Kingdom these had to be secret gatherings. Here each one who had known Meaning would receive a special cleansing from Word to wash away the marks of Branding. Then with a different understanding of context, Meaning, punctuation, enunciation and so forth, it became possible for the Meaning Speakers to grow in insight and clarity and each discover their own giftedness and special purpose for which they were created.

After turning from the mirrors, the Meaning Speakers often didn't know what to do because Misunderstanding abounded. It was necessary for them to ask for Guidance and Comfort from Union every day because with every Misunderstanding their sorrow increased. But so did Wisdom, the whispered Thought of Union. This was the way with Union: with every pain given to Him, the greater the joy that was returned.

The great thing about Union was that within Him the calculations for all possibilities were worked out, and so they were able to stay ahead of the game. Special envoys were sent out from Union called Archetypes – Significance and Satisfaction were the two bravest, and they in turn employed special helpers – Metaphor, Symbol, Analogy, Translation, to name but a few.

It was only the Meaning Speakers who were able to keep alive the ancient art known as Scripting, and for this they were given a guide – a book known as Script. This book contained many pages of heroic acts, suffering and tales of sacrifice as well as of great joy. When the words contained in Script were understood and spoken out by the Meaning Speakers, flashes of light in the shape of swords appeared. Media King hated this, and would put on special light and laser shows to distract too many people from seeing these flaming swords of light. The joy the Meaning Speakers shared with Union was very great indeed, as there were always some who saw these swords and so experienced the Moment of Clarification when the light was divided from the darkness. This was able to happen because of the Moment of Division, something many believed to be only a legend, wishful thinking or sheer folly.

However, they were wrong about this. It was at the moment of separation between light and darkness that Media King's message was seen to be a lie and, for a short time only, the ability to read the hearts of the Meaning Speakers was given. If the choice to tread upon the Path of Meaning was not taken at this time, Media King was able to reinforce his message, and after the Great Closure, heard as one clap of thunder in the skies, the darkness would deepen, each man seeing only himself, projecting only his image, living for himself and dying in fear.

January 2002

Return

Sorrow that cannot be spoken to, falling rain will wash away
Beauty that cannot be seen, the melting snow will reveal
Truth that cannot be heard will find its voice as the wind blows
Goodness that cannot be felt will be carried from the cold north
on a bird's flight
And strength, love, rest, home, will be on that wing

Psalm 72 vs 5–7

1998

Jesus' House

My feet will tread through yours
As you go forth this hour
My hands will reach through yours
As you minister the Spirit's power

I am the Alpha and Omega
The centre and the source
I am the temple and the ground
A mighty death-defying force

The cornerstone is not destroyed
The foundations still remain
I am the King, I am the Lord
Yesterday, today, tomorrow, the same

Malachi 4 v. 3
Hebrew 13 v. 8

2007